WISDOM
WORDS
OF
POWER

VOLUME 1
AJ WELCH

To order additional copies of this book, contact:
Xlibris
844-714-8691
www.Xlibris.com
Orders@Xlibris.com

ISBN: Softcover   978-1-6641-8980-5
        Hardcover   978-1-6641-8981-2
        EBook   978-1-6641-8982-9

Print information available on the last page

Rev. date: 09/09/2021

I started these Quotes and Sayings back in the year 2016 (December 23rd) and throughout the years, as a way to express my thoughts on actions, energy, beliefs, and at times internal feelings on living life. I wrote these thoughts down as a way of therapy for myself, and how I think about things. I can say with the forty years on this planet, I have seen a lot and heard a lot and experienced a majority of things, or had those experiences from others around me, physically and verbally. Being from New York's largest city, New York City, I was born in the 80's and raised through the 90's in the five boroughs. I Lost My Mother (Erlene Stanford) when I was three years old and recently lost My Father (Adolph Welch, Sr.) at the age of thirty-nine years old. In those regards, This Book is a Special Dedication to them, and all my other loved ones I lost. In recognition, Shout Out to my whole family and friends, all believers, and all my supporters. Not in a million years, did I ever think that I could be the author of my own book. This work was formed and decided to be put together with the intentions to inspire, motivate, and help others, no matter who you are. There is POWER in WISDOM!

Money is Everything
but Not Everything

Experienced without
being Experienced

Out of Sight
Out of Mind
Away from Family
Hardly Kind

No Evolving
through
Comfortability

In the SlaveShip??
What am I Doing!!

Respect...but don't care

What goes Up
Comes Down
What stays Down
Comes Up
What goes Left
Will go Right

Do not really eat Good
When the Hunt
is for No One Else

Part A
A Key Word to Life
Is Prevent
"Prevent from..."

Angels do more
than can be
Imagined

Right paths...
Opposites approach

Negativity trails Positivity
behind it
vice versa
Positivity trails Negativity
behind that

Actions speak louder
than words
Money speaks louder
than actions

Laugh Now
Cry later
Cry now
Laugh Later

Boredom could be
a blessing in disguise

Watch What You
Eat

Money attracts Money
Freedom attracts Freedom
Opposites do not attract
The Same attracts The Same

Part I
Timing is everything
and everything
is Time

GOD is a Witness
Believe GOD is Witness
for the work put in for
what is what and for when is when

Only what the hands
give does anyone care

Asian-African Ancestral
and Native American
Ancestral Smoke as...

Free at Last really
means to keep getting
real money at last

Take from those doing
better and also from those
Aspired Lifestyles Desired

Point-Blank
period
Sex always
Sells

Silence is Golden;
Quietness is GOD'S
Sound

Fear - Brokenness- Misery - Tiredness
loves company
Do not ever Become the company
of fear - brokenness - and misery - tiredness
So Kill and Destroy All Three and Four in
any Type - Way - Shape - Form - or Fashion

There is Strength
In Numbers
And
Power In Letters
Alone? No!!

Stay In School
Is Cool
But Not Ever
The Miseducation
of thyself
is cool to stay inside
      knowledge of self

Frustration is like
Incarceration to the
Psyche of the Mind
      Escape that Trap

Power means nothing
without Demand
Smart means nothing
without Supply
Sorry means nothing
without Laughter that is
behind that
Kings means nothing
without Queens
Life means nothing
nothing
without Peace and Love

Hear - Listen - Act - Do
Everything Oneself
Believes and Trusts
In - No Matter What

What Goes Around
Comes Around
In the same Measurement
Given At a Higher Degree
Done

Without Mom - Girl
or GrandMom...
Gets Hard and Harden

Push for change as
let things change
on GOD'S TIme and
leave things In GOD'S
Hands like Seasons To
Time Not Ever Man To
Date

Looking down to
Reflect on what went
Up
            It's a Matter of Time

Any City In the World
is A Song but - Especially
from the Home of Reggae
- Dancehall and Hip-Hop -
Rap incuded with Soca and
Calypso Culture and Latin
Culture

Because Anything is
possible Everything
can change

Money comes In
Girls come In
Money goes Out
Women go Out

The Game Of Life is like
Sports professionally
Be where there is More,
Cheers, and More Winning
for Oneself and Team
than be where there is less,
losses, and more losing
                    play it that way

    POWER
Is not a show
Is not a book
it's Real Life
Everything is,
and, comes from
    POWER

The Spirit of GOD
does Things Good
for Great and Makes
Things and Ways Happen
In Mysterious Ways
            GOD KNOWS BEST
            When left for Dead
            The Devil is a Lie

Life are for Those that Choose it,
Fight for it, Celebrate it, or Go after
it, But Death Understanding for, is
for everyone

Everything and Anything
that is said verbally and
done physically has a countereffect,
counteraction, and counterattack
through and with Motion and Energy
In Life
              from The Little to the Big Things

Sounds Never Ever Die
Therefore Our Words
Never Ever Die But
Travels Muffled Out Into the
Universe and Galaxies
Forever like Our Souls
                From Babies - Creatures
                Insects - Flowers to All
                Living Things on Earth

Man does not want to
See or Hear Man with More,
Do or Doing Better, or Be Equal
to that Man
Women are behind Men for
Freedom and Happiness
      Survival Existence
      Get and Have Things
      and get rich and wealthy
      while still young too

Everything In Life comes
In pairs of Two Meaning
It Always has the Opposites
of it
      Life
      Comes
      In
      Two's

Part I
The Energies at home or where
stayed, or past can/can't/will/won't
attract to the things being done and
life leads to the/those situations
                    Break this - that
                    or It with All Might

Those and the ways Family
Parents or Grandparents choose to treated
Sons and Daughters or Grandsons and Granddaughters
people of the world would have and will have the
tendencies to treat them the same way with both the
Negative (Get out of that - don't let them do the negative
ways) and Positive ways
So just imagine having to had - No Family - No Parents -
One Parent - No GrandParents - Or No One For You -
And Life is still a Bitch
Soft Love   Fathers look
Mothers   and want for their
want for their   children Survival
children Happiness   Hard Love

Can Be Thankful To Be
Somewhere But Not Happy
To Be There

> Which one comes before?
> Put Happiness before
> Thankfulness and Be
> Thankful To Be Happy

Part I
Do New Things
Different and New Results Shows Up
Do Things Not Ever Done
Get Things Not Ever Had
Get New Clothing and Footwear
Different and New Places Comes About To Go
Be Willing To Go Through Things
To Get What Is Wanted

> !!!!Get It!

Study More, Say More
Work More, Bank More
Be More, Get More
Know More, Change More
See More, Feel More
Hear More, Watch More
Touch More, Learn More
Taste More, Dislike or Like More
Do More, Have More
TIME EQUALS MORE
Moors   I   Native
                    American